Transition: A Collection of Poems

Rhys Milsom

ISBN 9781786155436

Dedication

For Emily and Ivy

Contents

Whispers of Home

The V of the green, burnt mountains meeting
My neighbour's garden, husky asleep
a blue wall, paint bubbles like freckles
The main road is empty,
the train tracks are, too,
sometimes the sun stays for hours
always, the grey clouds hover
The streetlamps are starting to splutter to life
like old car engines
Trealaw is slowing to a halt between
the V of the mountains
mothers are calling their children back home
Dewch adref ddiogel
Gyda'r lleuad

Generations

The Imperial mints jostle
inside the clear, glass bowl
and the crumbs of toast lie
upon the delicate cotton sheet.
My great-grandmother's
hair curlers on the floor, next to her chair.

The monotone radio voice,
like meditation practice
while the kettle boils,
rocking crazily on the boil
and her lighter clicks
as her knees do, too, as she
wanders into the kitchen.

The pigeons pass the window
like sleet
but don't come too close,
scared off by her emphysema cough
too shy to get lost in her
tobacco mist.

My great-grandfather's photo is everywhere,
alive even in death
the beige walls and carpets
mirror
her skin but not her:
calm
warm
tired

I was asleep
as my father drove me there
every time
waking up on her lap
I sometimes think it's
something I made up
but her antique telephone
in my grandmother's house
tells me
it was true.

Endear

The perpendicular crinkle of her smile
warms even the coldest crux
and can shift the frozen Himalayan
ice
cascading into snow
and on to villages, people, land –
a Pompeii of the other extreme –
frozen in their snowy glacial tomb

Yours

I would die for love
       like an ant killed by its queen
       opposite spectrums magnetised
       veering over and over, toppled and stuck
       eking away and out, away and out, wash over
       me, clean me like the tide
I would die for love
I would squirm and burn
I would run and run
I would pass over you, like the gulls
I would die for love

12 month routine

I run her a bath
in the little pink shell
watch as the water
reacts
to the bath lotion
half of it grows
into a glistening white afro
while the other half
lazily swirls there
like scum
stuck
to the sea harbour's walls
the window
is halfway open
the towels are
thrashing
against the wind
impaled to the line
with plastic pinches
they look like the flags
up high on the castle
when that hurricane from
America flirted with us

coaxing

her into sleep

is routine –

relax

quiet

bathe

eat

and she drops

off, easily

as our cat snoring

on the window-sill

with his forest of fur

belly

gently pulls in,

out

she kicks all the water

out of the bath

suds soothe into the carpet

like stock in broth

the teat is hungrily

gobbled

and soon she's asleep

her head sinks

into the pillow

and I wonder
if babies can dream
why can't I
anymore?

Llanon

I was down here once,
on the coast,
and on the bench
outside
the dayroom
was a single black feather
flesh, veins, sinew
hung off it
like rosary beads
component prayers
silently wailing,
unanswered
the bone was
matte silk
freckles
of blood
cresting like pools
on an empty landscape

I imagine the struggle
feather upon feather
vicious talons
bandy legs

beaks bred to maim
and kill
their contest
a labour of
ancestral breeding
and natural
omnipotence

The sea
whispers to the rocks
the air carries
her murmurings
to us and I try
to call back
but my throat seizes
the wind picks up
the birds are blown
from their path
and the tree limbs
tremble
and reach out
in agony

I pick up the black feather
and hold it to the wind
it snatches and
pulls it away
its trophy
to the appeaser
the hunter
the unforgiver
the sea.

EAJ

Amongst all the detritus
and debris
of my life
There is
a sanctuary where no darkness can get in

Like a lighthouse's eye
at night
clarity
sweeps away
the fog and
I see a passage
and escape

Like a ship
rotting with seaweed
and sea salt
I stay moored
in my passage
waiting for day to seep in
and for the birds to sing

You've seen me
at my worst
the hours
in the hospital
Waiting room
and psychiatric
assessments
but still you
stay, telling me
everything
is going to be OK
and wipe the sweat
from me
when I wake at night

Most people would
have gone by now
leaving me
drying out,
cracking,
like the Arctic
ice
as the sun
bleaches the bones
of fish that
float to the surface

Amongst all the detritus
and debris
you are the axis
you are my anchor
you are my purity
you are the birds
that sing
and remember
as you read this
I love you

Ochre

It's been two months
and it's still dead
adamant
not to bow to the process
that's intangible
that everything
succumbs to

Its roots
clutch down to the worms
and grip
like a limpet
stamped
to its grave

The fingers
reach out
in cramped derision
decorated with seeds, jewels
of fruits, shabby red
trophies
to the lizard-eyed
gulls and crows
squawking, scavenging
above
only to be thrown
to the ground
by the wind, their vehicle
as the scurvy
resin of the seeds
burns their bowels
and scorches
from the inside out

They'll be tossed
like newspapers,
wedged onto pavements,
pole-axed
to the concrete
car tyres screeching
over their wrecked wings

Through the coldest winter
in years
it still stands
crouched and sagging
against the brick wall
and peers
through the window:
a mute gatekeeper
that's watched things
only we know

Spring comes,
summer,
autumn,
winter again
yet the seeds remain
untouched, unripe
like a favourite place
in childhood

You're sure it'll never change
until suddenly, unnoticed
the brittle branches
hush to the grass
and get blown away,
auburn moss freckles
ingrain to sepia
like the teacher
in your favourite classroom
in a childhood
landmark

Dislodging the thoughts is as easy as learning to ride a bike

The ethereal blackout wasn't real
the pills weren't real
the midnight park gates weren't real
her fingers down my throat weren't real
the fizzing alcohol vomit wasn't real
the police car wasn't real
the nurse pressurising the syringe wasn't real
the Citalopram isn't real
the shadows at 3 p.m. weren't real
the boiling water on my hands wasn't real
the man peeking out the door frame wasn't real
the Olanzapine Teva isn't real
the constant scalp itch wasn't real
the bipolar, schizophrenia, psychosis wasn't real
the daydream tornado swallowing the black ball wasn't
real

the semi-colon tattooed on my finger isn't real
the eight month lay-off (poetry-less) wasn't real
climbing through the bedroom window wasn't real
the soap in my mouth wasn't real
the sleepless pain my parents endured, and
the worry that EAJ carried
the blankness that Ivy saw
transformed me into a fabrication
but now, that is all memoir
and this is non-fiction

What Would Kharms Say?

Snail shells, dirty mugs and buckets of rainwater all come crashing down from the eleventh floor. No one notices them before it's too late. They land on a Russian private eye, moon-lighting as a tramp, and kill him instantly. They find his head stuck in one of the buckets. He is given a state funeral and everyone cries apart from the man who lost his buckets.

Cashew-shaped petals

Cashew-shaped petals
turquoise and blue
wince and shudder
with each stamp of
her heel and his brogue
Their shouts and snarls
sting their lips and
stain their teeth
with birdsong
venom
Fluttering between the tantric
beige
each word and sentence
hangs and swings
like the abattoir's saw
Eventually crashing to the floor
scything the petals, crushing
their shells, like
octopus swallowing the crab
whole and helpless

Four rings are drowned
in the toilet bowl already
and she drops the fifth
in and scratches
his face, a
lace of blood above his cheekbone

The West coast of Wales

The rocks and pebbles
have been carried here
in the mothering arm of the sea
which also graciously shares
the wares of human consumption
and fragments of animals'
skulls, spines, shells, bodies,
wrinkle and fade away
on this shore, arching
on the West coast of Wales

A sign tells us not to litter
keep dogs on a lead,
beware of the tide.
But no one takes notice
they never have and never will
you hear about coastguard searches
and people never found,
missing,
broken and dead
washed up days, months, years later
amongst the rocks and pebbles
on this shore, arching
on the West coast of Wales

There's a small boy
playing amongst the fragmented landscape
his parents watch, drinking
wine and eating from a
battered picnic basket.
They shout and laugh at him,
his replies stolen and rushed
away by the wind
which makes our hair
sway like jellyfish legs
in the depths
The boy suddenly runs
closer to the sea
the wine pools onto the rocks
as his dad chases after his son
but he's already knee-deep
in the water
his dad stumbles and trips
leaving flecks of blood and
skin and
reaches for his son
just before he's
taken away by the furious, selfish sea
on this shore, arching
on the West coast of Wales

We sat and watched the whole thing,
on the wooden, chipped bench,
our hands interlinked
and feet touching,
I kiss her on the cheek,
softly,
the wind has frozen my lips shut,
we get up and walk back
to where we came from
on this shore, arching
on the West coast of Wales

Purgatory

It's another night
I lie
my thoughts cloudy
jittery

My consciousness
foggy
winter mornings
in the Ystradfellte woods

They're both asleep
the one-year-old
splashed out
in starfish pose

Her feet moulded
into the sleeping bag
her mother is
next to me

Whistles from her nose
and hot breath
flutters against my face
it reminds me of
the comforting warmth
of Spain or Italy
when you get off the
plane

All knotted up
bagged like sand
her fingers clutch
the blanket

Green painted nails
jut out
like the new daffodil bulbs
reaching out of the earth

I count the whistles
hoping for some
kind of flatliner
but it doesn't work

CBT

Walking along familiar streets
and the kerbs, they're cracked.
Heavy rain lashes on a window
and the rain blocks visibility.
The lightning, against the black,
the lightning is miles long, with sharp teeth.
I watch myself walk to the front door
I watch myself, but the door is locked.
The vortex, hovers and swirls
the vortex, hovers and swirls
the vortex, swallows me.

CBT II

Black fuzzy blocks shifting to the left,
other blocks try to slot in the empty space
but a landscape
bright with white light
is shown behind the blocks. A ribbon
appears, hanging off it is the keys to my car.
The keys to my car, I take them. I take the keys
and start the car
and then imagine crashing repeatedly
into another car, wedged sideways
now. Blocking my path as I keep driving.
I keep driving along the shore, the sand
covers the windscreen and a crack appears
groaning until the glass falls through
and I'm drowning in sand
I can't breathe.

Daydream

My mind wanders
amongst the jumble and
somehow
oddly
I think of lizards
and how they
twitch and dart
flash and scurry
through their lives

Their forked tongues
and blackberry eyes
manufactured
through thousands
of cells
organs
eggs
claws
nature

A chameleon
changes into the
colour
of its surroundings
just like water –
if a chameleon
is under water
what colour does it become?

What colou
                    r
Would I becom
                    e
Sprea   d
Under water?

Different Theories Mean Different Endings

He told me
cows are killed
in their sleep
but I know that's not true

Because the other
one told me
cows are shot
in the head
with a captive
bolt

And that's
a pretty big
way to go
out

But I don't think
cows mind at all
as they drag
their heavy bellies
through the fields
and grind the grass
to dust
in their sloppy mouths

When you next
see some
go closer
watch their

Eyes strain
sideways
and you'll see
the darkness

Of the night
split
by the cloudy
white

An Ode To City Road
(Or Somewhere Which Comes
To Mind)

Polish guy starts working in the
shop
tossing pizzas and churning out
pasta
painting the garlic bread
like an artist
making the final touches to an
exhibition piece

It all looks really good
the way he massages the Parma
ham
into the mozzarella
is pornographic
his tongue balancing
on his lips
as he rolls the meat over the
cheese

But however good his food is
it will never make it
because the Italian owner
with his red chef hat
tells him so

He also tells us *'don't trust the Turks'*
because his grandfather told him so
that they were horrible cruel
bastards
in the war

I ask him if he's ever eaten
mantı
and he says yes, *'a beautiful dish'*
and smacks his lips
blowing me a kiss at the same time

It's then I think
that whoever we are
Sometimes we're not meant to fit
in anywhere

Even in a country miles away
from home

Even in the war we didn't fit in
together
so what chances have we got now
on City Road
where there are more cultures
than streets

And more languages
than streetlights

Charles

It was only midday
but the sun
was sunk into the blue
smeared,
like burning treacle

Charles was telling me
about Jane
he really was
heartbroken
when it happened
but we all know
(or, at least, think)
he got over it in the end

The baby next door
keeps smashing
a spade onto
a plastic bucket
the sound doesn't echo
just sort of
stays there
like the sound

Of slapping
sea water
patted
on sand castles

The cat climbs
through the window
yawns
stretches his paws
tiny talons
scratch the table
he lunges forward
and starts to clean his belly
grunting with joy

I go
to tickle him
but he hisses
and sprints away
onto the fence
the wall
and out
of sight

I sit there
with the sun
hurling down
a bead
of sweat
drops
onto my arm
it becomes trapped
between the hairs

I look at it
at my hair
my arm
my skin
the sun

And head back
inside
to the sound
of Radio 6
where an African
drumbeat
plays

Right here
so many miles
(too many to count)
away
right here

Elocution

They said I should be proud
of my accent.
Its deep-reaching vowels
clawing at the dirt
coloured with my ancestors' blood.
Limping through the centuries with
knees curled like mountain tops,
my dulcet tones
confusing bone with born.
A grotesque mangling
of meanings and context
rendering my tongue
a shaman of insight
and confusion.

I want to rip it out
and grind
the words,
consonants, verbs, nouns.
Peeling against my weight,
rolling around like
oranges, fallen
from a market stall.
Their dull thuds
echoing my O's and A's.

They said I should be proud
of my accent.
And I am.
I sound like my father
and grand-father,
male lineage
coursing through my blood
and onto the next, the next,
the next,
who will not remember me.

I am proud of my accent.
Of the hills,
the mountains,
the churches,
the neglect,
the love,
the heritage,
the diminishing streets,
the familiarity.
I am proud.

Constitute

No walking on the grass.
Private parking only.
Failure to display a permit
will result in a fine
and your vehicle being clamped.
Visitors, please contact reception
or ring the buzzer at the entrance.

                    The grass is long now,
                it touches the door handle
                 and rests on the window
                which is cracked, dusty.
              Ornaments still stare back
              their eyes yearning for love,
        flies festering around their porcelain

One way only.
Give way to oncoming vehicles.
No right turn.
Caution: hidden entrance.
Maximum speed limit
of 20mph.

Water cries down
from the eyes of the mountains
and a pale blue,
luminous
moon hangs in the dark.
Dragonflies hide in the swamp
while metal and oil
amalgamate into one.

Sorry we're closed.
No entry between 8 a.m. – 6 p.m.
Respect our neighbours when
leaving.
Please leave the
premises quietly.
Alcohol is prohibited in
this area.

Face, sometimes,
the whirlpool.
It will hold you,
and drown you.
Heave off the pier and into the sea.
Watch the bridge burn,
the sun fall,
the rocks tumble,
the stars die.
Face, sometimes,
the whirlpool.

Scopophiliac

Have you ever wondered
if someone
is watching
the same raindrop
as you
when the rain is heavy?

When that raindrop
bursts
on the window
into thousands of tiny
other raindrops
and slides down

the glass
do you think
someone else hears
bullets being fired
or is it
just me?

A friend told me
that the rain
in Barbados
is worse than anywhere.
"You hear it before
you feel it

and it sounds like
grenades or your dreams
falling from the sky."
But I can't imagine
my dreams

falling from the sky
or falling from
anywhere
you can't reach,
because dreams
are in your head

and can't be touched,
like the rain
bursting
and breaking
against your cold
glass window

Acknowledgements

The biggest thanks goes to Emily, for putting up with me through the good, bad, and worst times. To Ivy, for making me kinder, more loving and, for being her dad. Without the two of you, this collection wouldn't have been written.

Thanks to Mam and Dad, Gran and Grampa, Jessica, Lisa and Mike, and Sally. Many of these poems are written about family, in one way or another, and you have all influenced me in some way – whether that be big or small.

Special thanks to Wynford, for being my 'supervising editor' for free and for the critiques, encouragement and writing space down on the coast of West Wales.

Bones, for being a *ffrind gorau*, and for being there.

Of course, thanks to Hazel and Anne at Accent Press for the edits, advice and encouragement when publishing this collection.